Teaching an Infant to Swim

Virginia Hunt Newman

Photographs by Robert Newman

Authors Choice Press
San Jose New York Lincoln Shanghai

Teaching an Infant to Swim

Authors Choice Press
an imprint of iUniverse, Inc.

For information address:
iUniverse, Inc.
5220 S. 16th St., Suite 200
Lincoln, NE 68512
www.iuniverse.com

Originally published by Harcourt Brace Javonovich

ISBN: 0-595-22324-9

Printed in the United States of America

*I dedicate this book
to my ever-loving husband,
who has been my constant
encourager and mentor*

Preface

Why write a book on teaching an infant to swim? Because I feel very strongly that there is a definite need for such a book, and the need increases as more pools are being built and more beaches are being used.

Ever since the day Mary Frances Crosby received her Beginner's Certificate and at age two became the youngest swimmer in the history of the American National Red Cross to do so, I have received letters from all over the United States and Canada asking for information on teaching infants to swim. I have even received telephone calls here at home in California from as far away as Connecticut from people who were seeking knowledge that would enable them to teach infants to swim.

Owing to the lack of written material on the subject, I felt I should share my knowledge with others, and add new hundreds to the number of children who each year learn how to begin a lifetime of health and pleasurable recreation in the water.

And if the material in this book saves the life of one child, I will have been repaid many times for the time and effort spent in writing it.

Contents

PART ONE

General Principles

1

Introduction

I have purposely written the greater part of this book as though I were talking to another swimming teacher in order to encourage the use of this tested and highly successful method of professional teaching.

However, you mothers—and fathers, too—who will take the trouble to pretend you are a teacher, and take the instructions literally and conscientiously, will have no difficulty in teaching your own child. It will be a pleasure, and give you a lifetime reward.

The first thing to establish is exactly what the infant is and is not going to learn. Let me say emphatically right here that I do not claim to teach a baby the crawl, backstroke, breast stroke, or any of the other formal swimming strokes used in or out of competition.

What the child will learn is the stroke that the American National Red Cross calls the *human* stroke, or, more descriptively, the crawl with a two-beat kick and underwater recovery of the arms. It is the one most commonly known as the "dog paddle."

He will first learn to paddle under water. Then, as he progresses, he will learn to come to the surface for a breath of air and go back under to swim some more. A group of little infants swimming together like this looks like so many happy porpoises disporting themselves alongside a steamship.

When the child has had sufficient water experience, he will be able to swim dog-paddle fashion on the surface of the water, going under only when he wishes to do so.

He will be able to recover an object from the bottom of shallow water, and in some cases from the bottom of deep water.

He will also be able to do a simple dive from the edge of the pool or a *low* diving board, and, of course, he will be able to jump into the deep end of the pool, and be able to float prone (face down) and on his back.

In other words, he will have attained the skills required by the Red Cross to pass their Beginner's Test.

But, more important, he will be *water safe*. He will be able to paddle himself to safety if he is pushed or falls into a body of water.

There has been much said, pro and con, on this matter of babies swimming. The most common objection is, "But they don't really swim." Well, in my opinion, anyone who can propel himself through the water, in any manner, is swimming. My dictionary says that to swim is to move on or in or over a body of water. It doesn't say that it has to be in the manner of the crawl, backstroke, breast stroke, side stroke, dolphin, trudgen, or any other way. For that matter, I have never seen a fish using any of these strokes; yet you can't deny that he *swims*!

My tiny pupils do not use any of these strokes until later on; but in the meantime they progress happily through the water, enjoying themselves, becoming healthier and stronger, and learning to preserve their lives.

Some say that babies forget. Take my word for it, they don't—a fact that will be discussed later in the book.

I have heard people say, "If parents did what they should, infants wouldn't need to learn to swim." They mean, I guess, that infants should be kept completely away from the water. How smug! But, unfortunately, it is not always that simple.

4

Friends of ours, Dr. and Mrs. Abner Moss, once had a back-yard pool with an eight-foot fence around it which they kept double-locked at all times. However, at a time when their daughter was not yet two years old, the pool man left the gate open once, and once the gardener left it open. Fortunately, Nanette could swim, and I know you could *never* convince these parents that she was too young to learn.

Even though parents are as careful as can be, there is that ever-present nagging worry that someone else won't be. You don't have to have a pool (or live by a lake), but you can't keep your neighbors from having one and being careless enough to leave a gate unlocked. Adults who don't have small children often fail to realize the dangers surrounding an infant that do not surround the older child.

Denise, a little pupil of mine, lived two doors from an apartment

The allure of the water is a very dangerous thing to a small child who cannot protect himself.

house that had a pool located just off the street, and the gate to the apartment opened into the pool area. Tenants coming and going invariably left the gate open. There sat a hazardous body of water, and not one tenant caring that there were at least a dozen children living in that block who were under three years of age.

Denise's mother was very grateful that she could swim, but the other mothers had to take matters into their own hands and insist that an automatic gate be put on the pool.

Most of the people who have closed minds on the subject are those who have never tried to teach a baby to swim—and many of them have never even seen one swim.

I again insist that an infant can be made water safe and at the same time build a strong, healthy body and have tremendous fun in the process.

What are the advantages of teaching an infant to swim? What is the best age to start lessons? How long should the lessons be? How long does it take? Do they forget? These are just some of the questions people ask me, and these, plus many more, will be answered here.

WHAT ARE THE ADVANTAGES?

Safety, health, and fun. According to the National Safety Council, more two-year-old children drown than children of any other age up to five! So, if a child is going to be exposed to water, he should be able to swim before he is two years old. Swimming helps develop a strong body, co-ordination, and a good appetite.

A good example of this is our little Patty, who was born six weeks prematurely with fluid in her lungs. Up to the time she was two years old, she was sickly and underweight. We still were giving her a bottle every morning at 2:00 A.M. With her doctor's permission, I started her swimming. The results were miraculous: she gained four pounds in three weeks, slept soundly through the night, and now looks like the healthy, strong child she should be.

Infants take to the water like the proverbial duck. I have never known a child who didn't like to swim unless he had been frightened or overexposed to the water.

WHAT IS THE BEST AGE TO START?

For whom? The child or the teacher? For the teacher, all other things being equal, a seven-year-old child is about the easiest. He understands clear explanations, and he has developed sufficient co-ordination to learn easily. In school he has had the experience of following instruction, and he has learned the discipline of being quiet and of listening. So, as far as the teacher is concerned, a child in the seven-year-old age group is just "ripe for learning."

As for the child, the age depends upon the individual. Some should start as soon as possible, perhaps at eight months of age. (Nathaniel Crosby started at four months.) Others can wait until they are seven years old. It depends wholly upon when the child is going to be exposed to the water. If he is going to be near a pool or a lake or the ocean, he should certainly be taught to swim at a very early age. The best time to learn to swim is *yesterday*.

HOW LONG SHOULD LESSONS BE?

Approximately one half hour. However, sometimes the infant will be cross or unhappy because he doesn't feel well or because it's an "off" day (we all have those); so he should be taken out of the water even if he has been in only five minutes. Some babies seem to get cold much faster than others. At the first sign of discomfort, you should take the baby out of the water. Occasionally a baby will be especially happy and having a wonderful time. Then it is all right to let him stay in the water for perhaps forty-five minutes, but no longer.

Example: An eighteen-month-old boy I was teaching didn't want to swim one Monday morning when I arrived to give him his lesson. His mother said, "Gee, I don't know what's the matter; he was in the water for *two hours* yesterday and had a ball!" I couldn't get him interested in swimming again for three weeks. So be sure to explain to parents that a small child can be exposed to undirected water play to an extent that will be detrimental to his learning how to swim. As the teacher, you'll have to be the judge, but it's a good idea to end the lessons just before he wants to get out, so that he will be eager for, and look forward to, the next lesson.

Our twelve-year-old son, Eddie, has enjoyed the story of the wife who serves her husband beans on Saturday, only to have them pushed aside. "What's the matter?" she demands. "Monday you ate beans, Tuesday, Wednesday, Thursday, and Friday you had beans. Now, all of a sudden, how come you don't like beans?"

So use, as they say, the first law of show biz: "Leave 'em wanting more."

HOW FREQUENT SHOULD LESSONS BE?

Ideally, every day, or twice a day, but at least three times weekly. (If the infant swims twice daily, the lessons should be limited to twenty minutes.) A child who swims daily will learn twice as fast as one who swims only three times weekly. Since a baby grows so rapidly physically and mentally, the less time between lessons, the better.

Consistency is also very important. For instance, it is much better for a baby to swim three times weekly every week than to swim every day for a while and then be out of the water completely for an extended period. I once knew a mother who would bring her baby every day, then get behind in her work at home and not show up at the pool for several weeks. We finally worked out a system whereby she planned three lessons a week and came extra times if she could. The scheduling and planning worked out very well, and the baby progressed more rapidly—even though he wasn't spending as much time in the water.

HOW LONG DOES IT TAKE?

The child's age must be the first consideration in determining how long it will take for him to become reasonably safe in the water. Generally it takes up to six months for a child under twelve months and up to three months for a child over that age. In actual time spent in the water, it will take from fifty to one hundred hours, depending on the age of the child. An eight-month-old will take up to one hundred hours, and a two-year-old can easily learn in fifty hours.

Another consideration should be the frequency of the lessons. As I said before, a child who has short daily lessons will learn to swim twice as fast as one who has three longer lessons weekly.

Because this method of teaching is unique, there is no way to guarantee parents that a baby will learn a certain amount in a given time. If you follow this method, however, parents can be assured that the child will have no traumatic experiences and that he will love the water all his life. (Many young children learn to swim by other methods—but they often hate it the rest of their lives.) Enjoyment of the water is more important than length of time, so don't try to push or rush the baby into swimming.

By "reasonably safe," I do NOT mean that a child could or should be left alone in the pool area for even a minute. I mean that if he falls or is pushed or jumps into the water, he can and will have the ability and the sense to propel himself to safety.

Within a few miles of my own home, there are at least three children alive and happy today who would have been swimming-pool casualties had it not been for their ability to remove themselves from the water. One instance was one-year-old Gary, who fell in the pool fully clothed as his mother sat reading with her back turned. Her first awareness of the event came when the thoroughly drenched and dripping small boy ruefully plucked at her sleeve saying, "Mommy—I fell in!" She has had many days to enjoy her child since, reflecting during every one how different her life would now be if that child had not learned when he did to *propel himself to safety.*

Two-year-old Craig watching movies of himself in the water with me taken the previous summer. He was thereafter eager to resume regular lessons. This technique was found helpful by his mother with an older brother, who had learned to swim before he was two but who insisted at the beginning of the next summer that he did not know how and would not try. She had then shown him movies of his swimming the previous summer, and he had immediately gone into the water and emulated himself perfectly. Children do not really forget how to swim; they sometimes just need reminding.

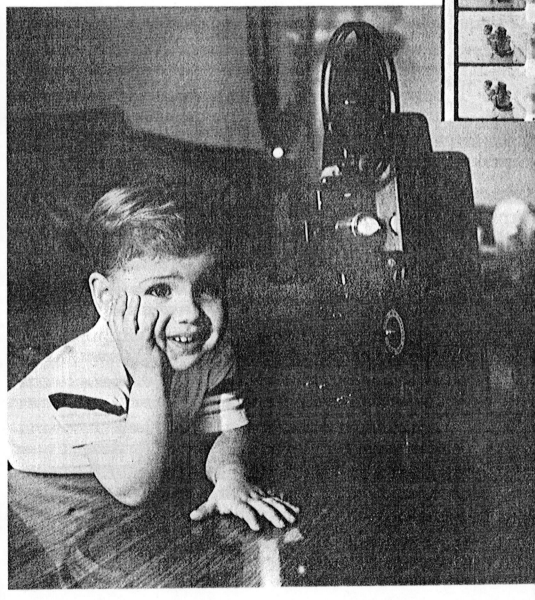

DO THEY FORGET?

Babies don't "forget" if you don't expect them to begin where they left off after being out of the water for six to eight months. You know that you yourself are a little rusty and out of form during the first weeks of a new swimming season. This is the main reason that *more than half* of all drownings that occur during the summer happen during the first few weeks. If you play golf or go to school, you know it takes a bit longer to adjust after a long vacation.

Infants have the same problem. If at the beginning of a new season you take the time to review, very carefully, everything the infant has learned, he will be at the stage where he left off in about two weeks. Then you can go on from there. Such a review is of the utmost importance.

ARE THEY AFRAID?

Babies are not born afraid of the water. They are not even born afraid of fire! (Loud noises are another matter—I'll talk more about that later.) Any fear of the water an infant has is acquired through example or a bad experience. The words "Now stay away from the water" have a familiar ring—and rightly so. If a child hasn't learned to swim, he must learn to have respect for the water, respect that requires keeping his distance. But what a shame! There is a better way.

If the infant cries while in the water, take him out and try to find the reason for his crying. He might be tired, hungry, or uncomfortable. Perhaps the glare of the water is hurting his eyes, or maybe his suit is binding. Sometimes, when you submerge him, a baby will swallow a little water or air, making a bubble in his tummy. If you burp him, he will be all right. But don't assume automatically that he is afraid of the water. He isn't!

WHAT ABOUT PROGRESS AND REGRESSION?

In all phases of learning, juvenile and adult alike, we learn in spurts. We progress for a while, then we stand still for a while until we start progressing again. In education, these standing-still places are known as "plateaus of learning." In teaching very young children, these plateaus are very pronounced. A child will progress for a while—perhaps very rapidly—then you will notice that he seems to be standing still or even regressing. He is on a plateau. It's as though he stopped to get a breath of air and take in all he's been learning. *Don't* try to force him. And, more important, *don't become discouraged yourself* (remember, he reflects your attitude) no matter how long he is in the regressive stage. He *will* suddenly start improving. All at once it will seem unbelievable that a child could improve so much overnight. It will be as though he's been saving up all his learning to surprise you in one day.

I once taught a little boy who, after having been on a plateau for four weeks, in just one day "recovered" (took a breath after coming up from submersion), floated on his back, and dived into the pool for the first time. Then he continued to progress with each lesson until he reached another plateau.

Parents must expect this unevenness, whether they plan to teach the lessons themselves or have their infants taught by a professional. Anticipating these plateaus before they are reached will spare a lot of anxiety.

HOW IMPORTANT IS YOUR ATTITUDE?

Nothing is more important than your cheerfulness and confidence. An infant will reflect your every mood, so be sure not to show any feeling of discouragement or lack of interest.

Infants display the canny instinct of a dog in sensing your true feelings. You cannot hide them.

Evaluate your own mood and strive to improve it. I have noticed on several occasions that when I have unavoidably had an "off" day, my small students don't seem to swim as well as usual.

WHAT ARE THE "BIG THREE" FACTORS NEEDED FOR SUCCESS?

The three most important factors in teaching the infant to swim are:

1. Demonstration
2. Repetition
3. Praise

A child must first know what he is expected to do. Swim for him. Let him observe other children swimming. Move his arms for him and kick his feet for him. In this way he will be able to get a mental picture as well as the "feel" of the motions of swimming.

Repeat and repeat and repeat and repeat, and then repeat some more. The lessons must be a repetition of the same thing, at the same time and the same place, day after day, week after week, for the very best results.

Don't underestimate the power of praise! The smallest infant or animal will respond to a friendly tone of voice when he doesn't even understand a word that is being said to him.

Praise can be used as a reward when the child does what is expected of him. My husband, Bob Newman, a motion-picture producer, once made a very successful and unusual TV commercial with a live rabbit that had been trained to pick up several silver dollars and put them in a bank. The rabbit was taught by being rewarded after each try. At first, of course, he could only smell the money, but he was rewarded with food every time he approached it. Little by little, after almost four months, he would go through the entire performance of picking up the silver dollars and putting them in the bank, after which he was rewarded with food. Many other animals that were once considered untrainable—for example, chickens—have been taught tricks by the use of reward. Pavlov, the great Russian psychologist, demonstrated the effectiveness of this principle many years ago in his famous experiments on "conditioned reflexes" in dogs.

A modified form of this method can be used in teaching babies to swim. Of course, we are not suggesting you withhold food from a child until he performs, but you can substitute praise—which is even better. When a child succeeds in doing what you want him to do—for instance, when he goes under water—praise him highly. Be excited about his accomplishment, act as though it is marvelous. You might say, "Oh, that's wonderful. I'm so proud of you, Mary." Children want to please, and they always respond to praise.

They want to give it, too. One day I sat a little group of my two-year-olds on the step, and said, "Ginny is going to show you how to pull your arms." When I came up, they all clapped their hands in unison and tiny voices said, "That's it, Ginny. You can do it. We're so proud of you."

Never appear disappointed if the child fails. As he progresses in his lessons, you will be teaching him things like recovering a poker chip from the bottom of the pool. There will be times, at first, when he fails. When he comes to the surface without the chip, smile and say, "That's fine, Johnny. You *almost* got it. You'll get it next time."

By accentuating the positive, you will make him eager to try again. Then when he does succeed, be sure to make him think it was the greatest thing ever!

2

Parents as Teachers

The following excerpt from Herman Melville's *Typee*, published more than one hundred years ago, gives an account of babies swimming in the South Seas. This is food for thought.

One day, in company with Kory-Kory, I had repaired to the stream for the purpose of bathing, when I observed a woman sitting upon a rock in the midst of the current, and watching with the liveliest interest the gambols of something, which at first I took to be an uncommonly large species of frog that was sporting in the water near her. Attracted by the novelty of the sight, I waded towards the spot where she sat, and could hardly credit the evidence of my senses when I beheld a little infant, the period of whose birth could not have extended back many days, paddling about as if it had just risen to the surface, after being hatched into existence at the bottom. Occasionally the delighted parent reached out her hand towards it, when the little thing, uttering a faint cry, and striking out its tiny limbs, would sidle for the rock, and the next moment be clasped to its mother's bosom. This was repeated again and again, the baby remaining in the stream about a minute at a time. Once or twice it made wry faces at swallowing a mouthful of water, and choked and spluttered as if on the point of strangling. At such times, however, the mother snatched it up, and by a process scarcely to be mentioned, obliged it to eject the fluid. For several weeks afterward, I observed the woman bringing her child down to the stream regularly every day, in the cool of the morning and evening, and treating it to a bath. No wonder that the South Seas islanders are so amphibious a race, when they are thus launched into the water as soon as they see the light. I am convinced that it is as natural for a human being to swim as it is for a duck. And yet, in civilized communities, how many able-bodied individuals die, like so many drowning kittens, from the occurrence of the most trivial accident!

As I have said, this book was purposely written as though I were talking to another swimming teacher, but you the parent are in a far better position than a stranger to teach your own infant to swim. Why? From the day you brought him home from the hospital, he has depended upon you for his very life and comfort. You feed him, you bathe him, you dress him, you play with him, you nurse him when he is sick. So he will accept the experience of swimming from you as a natural part of his life, just as he accepts all the rest of your tender loving care.

Parents—even parents who have been competitors themselves—who shy away from the teaching task do so for the most part because they think they have to know how to teach the swimming strokes to teach a baby to swim.

You don't need this knowledge any more than you need a degree in medicine to take care of your baby when he is sick; any more than you need to know all about bone and muscle structure to encourage him to walk; or any more than you need to know what makes a car engine work to drive to the corner drugstore to get his vitamins!

As I have pointed out, you are teaching the child to "dog paddle," and using his natural instincts to do so. Therefore, knowledge of teaching the formal swimming strokes is completely unnecessary.

It is, of course, better if you are a fairly good swimmer yourself. So, if need be, take a few lessons to strengthen your own ability, for reasons that are obvious.

Since being in the pool with your baby is tantamount to swimming alone, I would suggest that you never take him in the water without someone else being present—even a five- or six-year-old child—just as you would never swim alone without someone near to give assistance or to fetch someone else who could assist you if the need arose.

ABOVE: Mary Frances Crosby at eleven months after she had been swimming three times weekly for about six weeks. Although she can barely come up to get a breath of air, she would have been able to paddle herself to safety had she fallen in the water.

BELOW: Two-year-old Mary Frances Crosby is here as water safe as a toddler can be.

Remember, by swimming alone with a baby you are taking the chance of a double drowning—yours and your baby's.

As is many another common-sense rule for health or safety (dieting, using seat belts, etc.), this precaution is perhaps occasionally disregarded, or not taken seriously.

Swimming is not dangerous in itself. Neither is flying an airplane. But in both, there are conditions that are hazardous—for a minor mishap, if it occurs while you are not in the presence of at least one other person, can escalate into a serious tragedy.

So keep your co-pilot handy, and if it turns out that you never need him—why, that's just fine. Then you'll keep your child's swimming the delightful, safe, and rewarding recreation that it is. Just don't take unnecessary chances!

If you decide to teach your own infant to swim, start with the bath. When my son, Eddie, was only three weeks old, I got into the bathtub with him and played with him in the water. Even at this tender age, he instinctively held his breath when I momentarily submerged him, and he was never squeamish about having his face in water.

To use the bath as an introduction to swimming, fill the tub about two thirds with tepid water. Taking a few toys, get in the tub with the baby and play with him as he sits on your lap. Let him splash around to get his face wet. Playfully put your cupped hand full of water over his face. When he likes having water in his face, you can submerge him momentarily. An easy way to do this is to hold him under the arms, facing you, and dip him in the water for *one half second.*

When he is old enough to sit alone securely, you can let him play by himself. You will have to sit right beside the tub, however, because he will fall over in the water and you'll have to pick him up. *Never, never, never* leave him in the bathroom with a tub full of water even if he isn't in it. Children, especially toddlers, have a way of finding trouble.

Be sure to take his bath toys with him when he progresses from the bathtub to the pool, so that he will associate the fun of the bath with the new location.

I would also suggest to parents, whether you teach your infant to swim or let a professional teacher do it, that you discuss the matter with your family doctor or the child's pediatrician. Every doctor I have met thinks swimming is the most healthful sport there is, and your own doctor will probably think it is a wonderful opportunity for your child, but he may have reasons for not wanting your particular baby to swim at a given time. So, for your baby's own protection, ask your doctor first.

Parents who have had the experience of teaching their babies to swim have found it a very gratifying one. If you follow the instructions in this book and always use your own good judgment, you will have the same wonderful experience.

3

Preparing for the Lessons

Teaching an infant to swim is ninety-five per cent psychology! In fact, you can actually "teach" him very little. By exposing him to the water and using encouragement and praise, you give him the opportunity to learn. If a baby were placed in the water often enough, he would learn by himself to swim, through experimentation and observation, without instruction from anyone. Of course, it would take considerably longer, and his style might leave much to be desired.

A good friend, the late Virginia Hopkins, learned to swim at age two by merely imitating the older children she saw swimming in the Atlantic Ocean on the Florida coastline. She afterward became one of our country's best competitive swimmers and, later, a coach at a large metropolitan athletic club.

To prepare an infant for the experience, if it's possible, let him observe for several days before taking him into the water. This will give him the opportunity to see what others are doing and will help him get acquainted with the surroundings.

At age six months, Pilar and John Wayne's youngest daughter, Marissa, had her first lesson by watching her big brother Ethan swim. Then, sitting on my lap, she learned how to "pull and pull" with her hands and "kick and kick" with her feet. As the lesson was ending, Ethan accidentally splashed water on her while he was playing on the steps. Splashing while playing is an excellent way to help the infant get used to the water.

Have the parents bring some of the child's *favorite bath toys,* to help him associate the fun of his bath with swimming. See that his swimsuit fits comfortably, is durable, and is one he will not outgrow for at least three months. He should wear this same suit at each lesson for as long as possible. Infants become distracted by the slightest thing, and even the change of his suit could distract him so much that you couldn't get his attention.

I had this point proved to me very dramatically the first time Bing Crosby came to see his children swim. Ten-month-old Mary Frances and twenty-two-month-old Harry were ready to show off for Daddy. The morning of the big event arrived, and Bing came all the way from his home in Beverly Hills to the pool at the home of Dr. Abner Moss, in North Hollywood. Unfortunately, the children had arrived without their swimsuits. They were told it would be all right to swim in their underpants, but Harry refused to get in the water and started to cry. He was joined by a wailing Mary Frances. I didn't want them to be upset, so I said, "It's all right; you don't have to swim. Daddy will come another day when you have your swimsuits." The next time their father came to see them swim, they had their suits and were especially eager to swim for him.

Your own swimsuit should be one that you also can wear at each lesson for several months. I have found that a one-piece red suit works wonders with children. Red is the color most children recognize first and is usually their favorite color. Its use lends an air of fun and festivity to the lessons.

Light plastic poker chips are a wonderful help in teaching babies to swim. Their size is just right to fit into a child's hand, and they can be picked up easily. On the other hand, the child cannot break one or swallow it. He will first learn to pick these chips up as they float on the water; then he will learn to dive for them. All children throw things, but they will never hurt others or be hurt by a plastic poker chip no matter how hard it is thrown. Use the red and the blue chips. The white ones are too hard to see in the water.

WHAT YOU DO NOT NEED

Because of the psychological factors involved, be as careful about the things you *do not* need as you are about the things you do need. You don't need:

1. His diapers (during free swimming—I will explain a special use for them later, when he is being supported by a rope). They are too bulky and absorb so much water that they weigh the child down. Babies seldom have accidents in the pool, and the diapers wouldn't do any good if they did.

2. Swim caps. Small children should not wear caps. In order to keep the water out, a cap must be too tight to be comfortable. Water gets in the ears, and the cap holds in the water. Without the cap, the water flows out freely. Besides the discomfort of the moment, water is very difficult to remove from small children's ears. (To keep long hair from getting in the eyes, the hair can be put in a pony tail.)

3. Ear plugs. Ear plugs keep the child from hearing you clearly, and your tone of voice will play a large part in teaching him to swim even though he may not know what you are saying. However, if the child's doctor has advised some sort of ear protection, then use lamb's wool, which repels water. Don't use cotton; it absorbs water! All in all, it is best not to put anything in the ears if you can help it—in order not to establish a bad precedent.

4. Jewelry. Children shouldn't wear small necklaces or pendants. In the activity of jumping up and down and into the water, such objects can fly up and get stuck in the windpipe as the child gulps for air. Although occurrences of this kind may be relatively rare, it is an easy hazard to avoid.

In addition, children should not be allowed to have candy or gum in their mouths while they are in the water.

Be alert if a child seems to be working his cheeks and jaws in an awkward manner. It might mean that a small piece of food from his breakfast or lunch has lodged between the gum and the cheek. This is normal enough—but if he is about to start his swimming lesson, it is wise to check. Such a particle could get swept into his windpipe by the action of the water. In short, remove any such particles from his mouth before beginning the lesson. You can usually tell if he has food in his mouth because he will play with it with his tongue.

5. Kooky-looking garb. Don't wear a swim cap—or hat, sun visor, sequined sunglasses, or anything else—that will make you look strange to the child. I have seen teachers wearing a frown and a getup of sloppy sweat shirt, dark glasses, and sun hat, trying to get an infant to stop screaming long enough to learn to swim, not realizing that the child was afraid—not of the water—but of this strange-looking creature who was manhandling him!

6. Oil on his skin. He will slip out of your hands.

7. Long fingernails. A small point, but important. Because children in these early years make very rapid movements, and because you will have to make some fast moves yourself, keep your fingernails short, so that you won't injure your little pupil. This precaution applies particularly to women teachers.

Note: I have gone into great detail here because you will find that paying attention to all these things can make it easier for you to be successful. *Then you will be properly using the instincts of the infant.* It could turn out to be more important than your own knowledge of swimming!

4

Use of a Rope and Towel

Very tiny children—those under eighteen months—are sometimes difficult to hang onto in the water, especially if you aren't used to handling
babies, and particularly the skinny, squirming ones. I have discovered
that using a towel wrapped around them with a rope tied to it makes it
easier to handle these "wily worms."

I happened on this harness purely by accident. When I first started
teaching the Crosby children, I couldn't keep Mary Frances out of the
water long enough to give Harry his swimming lesson. She'd cry to get
in the water with us all during his lesson. Since she was only ten
months old and he twenty-two months, I couldn't safely handle both
at once.

I decided to try a tea towel and rope, since they were the handiest
things around at the moment. So while I gave Harry his lesson, someone—Louie, the chauffeur, Mrs. Moss, or Mary Frances's mother—would
walk around the edge of the pool holding her with the harness while
she happily paddled in the water.

The tea towel seems about the easiest thing to use, other than a small
diaper. (My previous remark about the diaper does not apply here,
since it is now tied around his chest, and he is being supported by the

rope.) It is advisable not to use anything heavy, like a terry-cloth towel. It's too cumbersome.

Also, don't use old material that might tear and give way, and thus leave the child without support in the water.

The rope should be about five feet long and of a material that won't slip and come untied (as some shiny plastics do). Just a plain old clothesline you buy in the market is the best kind I have found. Be sure to get a rope that isn't rough, or you'll get little slivers in your hands. When your hands are wet and soft anyway, you can get a rope burn if the material is rough.

APPLYING THE TOWEL

First triple fold it lengthwise so that it is about four inches wide. Then wrap the towel around the infant's chest just under the armpits. Be sure that it is well above the tummy area; otherwise he will tip forward when you hold him. The towel should be wrapped around him in such a way that it isn't too loose, and might slip off, or too tight, so that he cannot breathe with ease.

Pin the towel to one side in the back. Use two diaper pins, one at the top and one at the bottom. One pin is not strong enough, and regular safety pins may come unpinned.

ATTACHING THE ROPE

Tie the rope to the towel in the middle of the back. This is important, because he will roll over to the side, off balance, if the rope is not tied in dead center.

I wasn't in the Navy, but somewhere along the line I learned to tie a square knot, and I have found that it does the most efficient job of staying tied. Ask your friendly neighborhood Boy Scout to explain the square knot—and how to tell it from a granny.

28

As with the swimsuit, always use the same towel and rope. You might not be able to tell the difference, but your little charge could. Each child should have his own equipment.

It should be your responsibility to see that the rope and towel are kept in condition to be usable and are available when the infant comes for his lesson. I have found it helpful to attach the pins to the end of the towel so they won't get lost.

It has been my experience that it is best to keep all the infant's equipment—suit, toys, rope, and towel—at the place where he is taking lessons.

(If you are teaching in a school, you might have a rack with each child's name over a hook for the rope and towel. A name on the wall even operates as an incentive or a status symbol. Many famous Hollywood restaurants—Don the Beachcomber's, for one—use it to lure back the movie and TV actors.)

I don't need to tell you that parents who are unfamiliar with swimming are great for forgetting swimsuits, etc. (Unless, of course, the parent plans to bring the baby already dressed in his suit.)

Don't put a *wet* towel on a baby. In the first place, wet material tends to tear when you put a pin through it. Moreover, you know how uncomfortable it is to put on a wet suit. If the towel is wet when the lesson should begin, put the baby and the towel in the water before applying it.

USING THE "HARNESS"

Wrap the rope around your hand so it won't slip out. Hold it just above the knot, because the baby is devoid of any balance in the water at this point. Gain the necessary leverage by resting your arm and elbow on his back.

It might also be necessary to support him under the chin at the beginning, until he gains balance.

Walk along in the water beside him holding him in this manner until

ABOVE: This picture shows how to rest your arm against the child's body to help him gain balance in the first few lessons until he can balance himself.

BELOW: This two-year-old is reaching out to get a poker chip that is floating on the water. This "game" helps him get the feel of arm movements.

ABOVE: As I walk along the edge of the pool and hold this little boy up with the "harness," he pulls and kicks as he reaches for poker chips floating along the edge.

BELOW: When the pressure on the rope is released, the child will submerge. After momentarily being under the water he should be brought up to the surface again. This is one of the ways to help him learn to recover.

he shows some indications of balance by relaxing and not wobbling.

Don't submerge his head when he is in the rope and towel until he is very familiar with having his head under water. He needs the security of being held in your arms when he is being introduced to having his face in water.

When you can submerge him while he is in this harness, be sure that his face is either all the way in the water or all the way out of the water. If a child's face is under the water so that his mouth is covered but his nose is not, he may try to breathe, thus sucking water into his nostrils. Although the presence of this water is not hazardous, it can be very painful.

In about three or four lessons, when he has good balance in the water and can hold his face out of the water without your supporting his chin, gradually use more of the rope. When you are using so much rope that you can no longer make leverage for him with your arm, you can then hold him with the rope as you walk along beside the pool and pull him.

As soon as the infant can pull with his hands and you begin to teach him to come up to get a breath of air, you no longer need the harness to help handle him. However, I usually continue using it because most children like to be towed around in it. Another advantage is that the parents can be encouraged to use the harness. When a child loves to swim, he doesn't care who is on the other end of the rope.

If the child resists when you begin to use the harness, don't use it. Most children under eighteen months will not resist, and most children over that age usually do resist. I don't know why.

Note: This harness is strictly for your convenience in handling a very small child; it doesn't do anything for your pupil at all. So if you don't want to use it, you're not denying the child anything he should have.

Now, let's get on with the lessons themselves.

PART TWO

The Lesson Method

5

The Beginning Lessons

Because of the vital importance of the beginning lessons, be especially sure that all the conditions are optimum.

BE SURE THE BABY IS NOT HUNGRY OR TIRED

The lesson should be at the same time each session—either in the early morning or after his afternoon nap. Toward late morning he begins to get hungry and tired.

Don't let him swim immediately after eating. Babies often vomit when they are jostled around soon after a meal. There is no medical proof that swimming just after eating will cause any ill effects, such as cramps, but a feeling of sluggishness does exist after eating a meal. (I mean a whole meal—not just a cookie or something like that.) Since such a lethargic state is not the optimum swimming condition for the infant, it is better to wait about an hour.

Swimming at the same time each lesson helps to provide the repetition that facilitates learning, helps form a happy habit, and makes his improvement easier.

GIVE THE INFANT YOUR UNDIVIDED ATTENTION

The closeness of your personal relationship will assure success only if you give him full attention, without distractions or interruptions. Don't interrupt the lesson to answer the phone or for any other reason, and don't distract him by conversations with anyone else—especially on a subject other than swimming. The infant's attention span is so short that the tiniest diversion will make him lose interest for the rest of the lesson.

EVALUATE EACH INDIVIDUAL CHILD

Keep in mind that there are specific differences in a child's physical development, co-ordination, and balance—which vary in individuals at different ages.

A baby's pattern of response to teaching, and his individual elements of swimming style, while following a general pattern, will exhibit definite individual differences, much as fingerprints differ for each child.

One infant may kick both his feet with froglike movements, and another will kick with just one foot and let the other one trail. One will pull with his arms at his sides while "finning" with his hands, and another will pull with his hands in front of him.

Baby girls usually learn more rapidly than boys of the same age because they are more advanced in co-ordination and balance. Although the boys don't learn as rapidly as the girls, they will be better than the girls later on.

Psychological experiments prove that a two-year-old monkey has a reasoning ability far beyond that of a human being of the same age. If a piece of candy and a banana are placed on a chandelier without any obvious way of reaching them, the monkey will use boxes, a chair, tables, or anything else available to reach the banana. The human baby is unable to reason this out. Later on, the monkey's intelligence levels off, whereas the child's continues to grow. When each has reached adulthood, the man has far surpassed the monkey in brain power. The same contrast is true in the physical development of boys and girls. The baby girl is more advanced than the boy. In adulthood most men are stronger and have better co-ordination and balance than women.

In a later chapter I will discuss the different ways babies swim and what to do to correct bad habits.

WATER TEMPERATURE

Out here in Southern California we keep our pools quite warm for teaching purposes. In this semitropical climate our blood is rather "thin," and we can't tolerate cold water very well. Most swim schools keep their teaching pools at about 90° Fahrenheit, because *any* beginner swimmer cannot move around enough to keep himself warm. This is especially true of the skinnier little kids, who haven't much meat on them. In at least three homes where I teach, the water is kept at 95°, and as incredible as it may sound, these children sometimes still get chilly.

I realize that in some sections of the country youngsters would be uncomfortable in water this warm, for two reasons. First, because they are used to freezing winters, which "thicken" the blood. And second, the air is not only very hot, but also very humid. Since the high humidity keeps the body from cooling itself, 90° water would be rather sickening and enervating to those who live in cooler climates.

Therefore, to arrive at the best temperature for your teaching pool, use these rules:

1. Take into consideration the local weather conditions, and their physical effects on the child.

2. Keep the infant comfortable at all times. Remember that he does not move enough to keep himself warm by exertion, yet water that is too warm has its ill effects.

3. If the water is not at the best temperature, shorten the lesson accordingly.

In places where the temperature of the water cannot be controlled, such as lakes or unheated pools, the lesson must continue only as long as the child is comfortable.

INTRODUCING THE INFANT TO THE WATER

If the infant is shy and doesn't want to go into the water, it is a good idea to have the mother or father take him in each lesson until he gets acquainted with you. I have often asked a parent to come into the water with us for the first dozen lessons, until I was sure the child would not be anxious without him.

At any rate, don't rush the child into the water if he shows any signs of reluctance, because you will meet only with more resistance. Try to find an incentive to make him want to go into the water.

Many times a child just wants to play around the pool for a little while. For this reason, ask the parents to bring him to the pool at least twenty minutes before his lesson. It will give him an opportunity to observe what the other children are doing, and he will be more likely to want to go into the water when the time comes. If you teach the child in his own home pool, ask the parents to let him play around the pool area for a little while before you arrive. Later on, this device won't be necessary. You might encourage him to throw his toys into the water; then he'll want to go in after them.

Sit on the steps with him or hold him on your lap and talk to him in a gentle manner, using his name. "We're swimming. Swimming is fun." Gently kick his feet for him in a flutter-kick motion and say, "Billy can kick, kick, kick." Pick him up and walk across the pool slowly while you continue to talk gently to him or maybe sing a nursery rhyme. On your way back to the steps, stop in the middle of the pool and go round and round with him, singing something like this little ditty:

The baby should play in shallow water to help him become acquainted with it.

Ring around the rosies,
Pocket full of posies;
Water, water,
We all fall down!

After saying "We all fall down," put your face in the water without submerging his face. When you come up, show him that it is a game by laughing and saying something like "Oh, that was a fun game!"

Some children become so delighted with this game that they will put their own faces in the water when you do.

An infant can easily become accustomed to moving in the water by walking in shallow water and picking up floating plastic poker chips.

A trio of two-year-olds sings "This is the way we wash our suits."

When you get back to the steps, float several poker chips on the water along the steps. Then, holding his hand, let him walk through this shallow water to pick up the poker chips. After each one he picks up, praise him and let him know that he is doing something that is good. If the child is an infant who cannot walk, hold him while he picks up the chips. The lesson should end now. Say to the child, "It's time for Billy to get out of the water. I had fun swimming with you today." The rest is optional, but I always play the following game. I take his swimsuit off and let him wash it up and down in the water while singing:

> *This is the way we wash our suits,*
> *We wash our suits, we wash our suits;*
> *This is the way we wash our suits*
> *Every swimming morning.*

Let him throw the suit out into the water; then take him out to get it. Later he will be able to recover the suit himself. Some parents are afraid of this game because they fear that their children will become immodest. As children get older they are naturally modest and will not want to take their suits off any more. The reason for removing the suit in the water is that the baby may be immediately wrapped in a towel or robe as he is lifted out of the pool and will not be exposed to cool air in a wet suit. Children love this game. If after you explain this to the parents they are still reluctant, skip the game. The parents' feelings are more important than the game.

One day when Harry Crosby was about three years old and we had played "This is the way we wash our suits," I told him it was time to get out. He replied: "No, Ginny, I want to swim in the nude for a little while." Two-year-old Mary Frances, who was swimming nearby, said, "Where is the nude, Ginny? I want to swim in it for a little while too."

You can look forward to the day when it's time to remove the suit of a child about two years old and he says: "Why don't you take off your suit too?" You can answer this one to suit yourself!

To get the child out of the water, bounce him up and down saying, "One, two, three, four—Billy jumps out of the water!" With this, put him on the edge of the pool or into his mother's waiting arms.

I have found this last game invaluable in getting them out of the pool. Once they are out of the pool after the lesson, never let them come back in the water, or you might find yourself with the problem of keeping them out.

Continue with these "get-acquainted" lessons until you feel that you have the child's confidence. This will take perhaps three or four lessons.

SUBMERSION

After one "Ring around the rosies" game, say to him: "Billy will play this time." When you put your face in the water, put his in too.

When an infant's face comes in contact with the water, even for a second, he will instinctively hold his breath. It's the same natural reflex action a child has when he automatically blinks his eyes if an object comes close to his face.

One of the greatest misconceptions is that an infant will breathe in when his face is in the water. As long as his mouth *and* nose are in the water, he will instinctively hold his breath. He may swallow a little water, but he won't breathe in. As I said before, he will try to breathe if his mouth is covered but his nose is out of the water. Then he might get water in his nose—and boy, that hurts! For this reason, it is very important that the child's face be all the way in the water or all the way out.

With older children, some teachers coax a squeamish pupil into putting his face in up to the chin, then the nose, then the eyes, until he will put his face all the way in the water—which is a way of learning that older children enjoy. But this method will not work with infants. You have to "take the bull by the horns" and submerge his face all at once.

His reaction may be one of pleasure, he may be startled, or he may cry a little. If he does cry, don't try putting his face in the water again, but laughingly wet his face with your hand full of water instead. After five or six lessons, he won't mind having his face in the water. Then you will be ready for the next step: the submersion.

There are some children who just do not want to get their faces wet, and you have a problem. These children 99 and 44/100% of the time are little girls over eighteen months of age who have been overprotected and too delicately handled all their lives. I solve this problem by first discontinuing all the lessons as such.

The "lessons" I use instead consist of *one* immersion under the water *every day* (even if their scheduled lessons are three times a week) if at all possible. After the submersion I put my hand out and let them hit me. This seems to relieve any frustration they feel from being overpowered. I always tease a little by saying, "Oh, you can hit harder

This two-year-old likes the gentle approach to getting her face wet.

than that." Then they look forward to the same opportunity the next day to see if they *can* hit harder. Depending on the child, it will take from one to two weeks.

When he will put his face in the water without fussing, I continue with the lessons as usual. I have found it inadvisable to try to continue lessons until the child will submerge, because the problem will have to be faced, sooner or later, and the sooner, the better.

I *do not* use the above method of teaching on a child who has had a bad experience and is afraid of the water.

When you submerge with him, the dip should be only *one half of a second.* Then you come up and say, "That was fun, wasn't it, Billy?" Submerge him only once and continue with the lesson. When you have repeated five or six more lessons with the submerging, you will be ready to let go of him in the water.

6

Opening the Eyes under Water, Independent Submersion, and Swimming

When the child no longer minds having his face in the water, you can begin to let him stay under for longer periods of time. During the "Ring around the rosies" game, begin to let him stay under a little longer with each dunking.

As a first step from the one half of a second you've been keeping him under, advance to one second. Then gradually increase the time to three, four, five seconds, and so on. You will have to be the judge of how fast you can increase the time of keeping him under the water.

Watch for signs of his wanting to come up. One such sign is that he will push his feet against your legs in trying to come up on his own.

OPENING THE EYES UNDER WATER

When he can stay under the water for five seconds, comfortably, begin waving to him under the water and smiling, or tap him on the nose or chin in a playful manner. When you come up, say: "I saw Billy under the water." These activities under the water will teach him to open his eyes while submerged. As he learns to swim, he should be taught to look out for other swimmers. (This is a long way off at this point, but it is important to keep looking toward the final goal.) Another reason he should keep his eyes open under the water is a psychological one, which can be shown in the following anecdote.

One day I received a call from an upset mother whose family had only recently moved into our area. She said that her three-year-old son, Greg, who had learned to swim from another teacher the year before (at age two), now had forgotten how to swim and seemed afraid of the water.

Could I teach him again? I agreed to do so, not yet knowing the real problem.

As I drove over to their new home I wondered what kind of a traumatic experience the boy might have had. Unfortunate encounters with the water are the most common cause of such fear in a child.

However, in the first "get-acquainted" lesson I learned that this was not the case. He had not had a bad experience that would account for the fear he displayed.

In playing and talking to him, I found out that he was afraid to put his head under the water because it was "dark under there." They had moved from a home in which Greg had lived all his life. It was in that family pool that he had learned to swim. Although he had always been under the water with his eyes closed, he had shown no fear of such completely familiar surroundings. Now, his timidity was merely a reaction to the darkness of the unknown.

I taught him to open his eyes under the water by placing red and blue poker chips on the first step of the shallow end of the pool. Then I said, "Which color does Greg want Ginny to get for him?" He chose a red one, and I put my face in the water and picked up a red chip to give him.

Then I said, "Now it's Greg's turn. Ginny would like a red one too. Be sure to open your eyes so you can see." He put his face in the water and came up with a red chip.

46

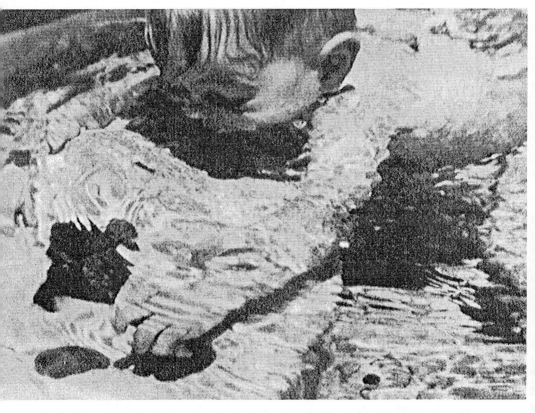

In the beginning lessons a fun way to get the child used to having water in his face is to let him fetch poker chips from under the water. This little boy is trying to get a chip from the top step of the shallow end of the pool.

From the shallowest step in the pool we progressed in this manner to the second step, the third, and finally to the bottom of the pool. At the end of three lessons, Greg was swimming as well as he had been at the end of the preceding summer.

His mother and father were both delighted and surprised. This is another good example of why you shouldn't assume the infant is afraid of the water without checking.

INDEPENDENT SUBMERSION

When the child can stay under the water comfortably for at least five seconds and can open his eyes under the water, you can start to let go of him in the water. When you let go of him, it should be when he is already submerged. If you let go of him and then let him slip down into the water, he might get the feeling of falling, and it could frighten him. I usually let go of him during the "Ring around the rosies" game. After "We all fall down," I go under the water with him. Then, very quickly, I let go of him momentarily, then grab him again to come up out of the water. Repeat this procedure until the infant is used to it—perhaps for four or five lessons.

Now after the "We all fall down," let go of him to submerge and go under yourself to get him and bring him to the surface.

Let's review to this point. The infant should be able to pick up chips that are floating on the water (walking along the step, if he can walk, or picking them up while you hold him, if he can't walk). He should be able to open his eyes under water, and stay under the water at least five seconds. (This is a very conservative limit; many children can stay under much longer.) And, finally, he should be able to be released in the water *before* he is brought to the surface. That's a pretty good start.

At the end of the lesson you can now add a new activity: picking up the poker chips that are placed *under* the water on the first step. Put six to eight chips on the top step of the pool and show him what you want him to do by putting your face in the water and picking up a chip. After putting the chip on the edge of the pool, ask the child to get another one for you. When he picks one up, be sure to praise him for his efforts.

When you start any new activity, it is a good idea to repeat it only once or twice during the lesson, just to give him the idea, then gradually increase the number of times you repeat. *Always remember that the span of attention of children in this age group is very short.*

End the lesson now with the "This is the way we wash our suits" game—if you have decided to use the game.

Now to get him out of the water, count: "One, two, three, four—Billy jumps out of the pool," bouncing him as you count and lifting him out on the count of four.

Note: Always count to the same number! Three, four, or five—it doesn't matter; but don't count to three one time, then five another time. The child will come to know that on a certain number he is going to go out of the pool. It gives the child a sense of security to know exactly what is going to happen to him—for better or worse (when he has to get out of the pool and doesn't want to).

Continue with the lessons given so far, gradually letting him stay under the water longer when he submerges, playing more games during the lesson, etc., for about four or five lessons.

Next, after the "Rosies" game, as you approach the steps, stop about two feet from the step and give him a little push to the steps, so that he can catch onto the top step. This is his first time to be completely free from you, so you must be sure to give him the reward of praise here, such as "Bravo! I didn't know you could swim all by yourself!" Each time you guide him to the steps, gradually start back a little farther, but be careful not to stand back too far, too soon. The child must learn to balance himself in the water before he swims too far alone, even though he can hold his breath long enough to swim quite a distance.

If he begins to tip from side to side or roll over, you have started him too far from the step.

At this point, I usually start taking him to other parts of the pool. First along the edge opposite the middle of the pool, then to the deep end, around to the other side, and back to the shallow steps.

To travel around the pool easily and safely, I float on my back, propelling myself by kicking, finning with my hands to guide us, and letting the infant sit or lie on my stomach. He can face you, you can see and talk to him, and, of course, you are in a position to grab him if he should start to go off on his own.

As we swim along our adventurous journey, we stop to see various

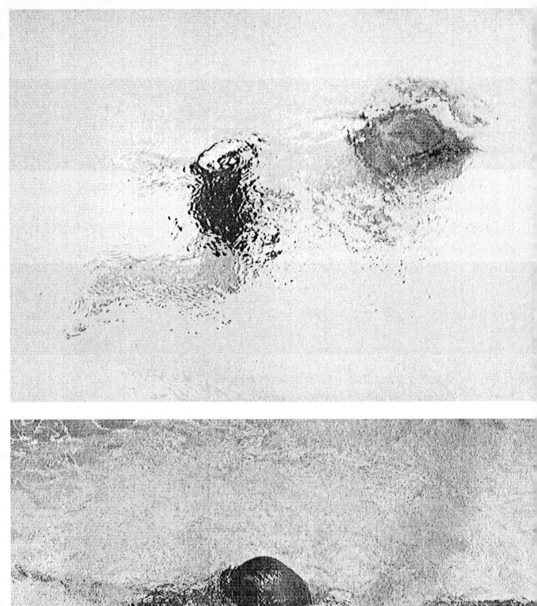

Here are ways infants kick. One is kicking with a froglike motion, another is kicking with one foot while the other drags behind, and still another is kicking with a bicycle motion.

sights around the pool, such as the skimmer. In the metal cover over the skimmer is a small hole used to pick up the lid. The sun often shines through and makes a ray of sunshine. If you put one hand over the hole, the ray goes away; remove your hand, and it comes back— just a little magic that children enjoy. Children also like to visit the thermometer. You can put it in their hands and let them look at it, and say, "The thermometer says Billy's water is very, very warm." You can make up your own stops on these adventures around the pool, and there are more suggestions in the chapter on games.

Besides adding excitement and fun to the lessons, the trips around the pools are valuable because it is important for a child to know the pool he is swimming in, particularly if it is at his own home. If he should happen to fall in the water, it will then be in a familiar place and he won't become frightened.

KICKING

When a child is submerged in the water, he will instinctively kick his feet in some manner. If he cannot yet walk, the kick will probably be one like that of a frog—both feet and legs working together, pushing back and forward. Sometimes he will kick only one leg in this manner while the other remains unmoved. As he approaches the walking stage and his co-ordination becomes more developed, he will have a tendency toward the "bicycling" of his legs, then finally the flutter kick.

When he is actually swimming in the water, I do not try to change his normal kicking motions, but when we are playing on the steps, I start showing him the flutter kick. To accomplish this, I put him on the step on his stomach and kick his feet for him in the flutter-kick movements and say, "Johnny can kick, kick, kick." Doing this kicking for him helps to develop the "feel" of the proper kicking motion and the co-ordination it takes to accomplish it.

Later on, when he can kick by himself, a child likes a game I call the "Animal" game. As you are kicking with him, say: "The duck says, 'Quack, quack'; the pig says, 'Oink, oink'; the rooster says, 'Cock-a-doodle-do,'" through all the animals you care to name. Children love this game. It helps them learn the sounds of animals and gives them an incentive to want to kick their feet properly.

Spending just two or three minutes on the steps in this manner each lesson is sufficient for your purpose. You will notice that as time goes on he will begin to use the flutter kick in his swimming.

PULLING WITH THE HANDS

A child usually does not pull with his hands instinctively, as he instinctively kicks his feet when put in the water. So here is one of the skills that he must be taught. He usually paddles his hands down by his sides when he first is introduced to the water. This motion of his hands does help to propel him forward, but he cannot easily "recover" unless he uses a pull in front of his body to help bring his head out of the water.

It is a simple matter to teach him to pull properly. First, sit with him on your lap, and pull his hands for him, saying: "Pull and pull and pull." This will give him the feel and the mental picture needed for him to accomplish the correct action of the hands. Then, holding him around the waist and taking him to the step, remind him to pull with his hands. When he is ready to swim out to you, be sure to remind him to "pull and pull and pull" just as he leaves the step.

As they learn the action of the hands, some children have a tendency to bring their hands out of the water. This should be discouraged. It splashes water, and they could suck some of it into their windpipes. Although this isn't necessarily dangerous, I don't have to tell you how terribly uncomfortable and frightening it can be.

Here are two different ways infants pull with their hands. One is pulling with his hands in back; the other is pulling with her hands in front.

As your pupil learns the proper movements for hands and feet, he will automatically put them together.

Now he is ready to learn how a swimmer must breathe—the art of "recovering."

7

Breathing–Learning
to "Recover"

Of all the skills the infant will learn, "recovering" (coming up to get a breath of air) is the most important. Since recovering is also the skill requiring the most co-ordination, the teacher should be prepared to devote extra time to its development.

After the child has become used to the water, at the beginning of the lesson, sit him on the step. Stand in the water about three feet in front of him, putting out your arms to encourage him to come to you. If he hesitates, pull him gently off balance to make him understand what you want him to do. As he falls forward, let him go under the water. After he reaches you, catch him by pulling him up out of the water by the chin. This is the first step in teaching him to recover. Be sure to praise him: "That was wonderful, Johnny!" Then continue with the lesson as usual. Each day stand a little farther back, being careful not to try to stand too far back too soon. The infant needs to gain balance before he tries to swim too far.

From this point on, until he can recover by himself, *always* pick him up by the chin when you bring him up from under the water. This teaches him to bring his head up to get a breath.

We are on the way—it won't be long now!

When he will come to you readily from the step, after you pick him up by the chin let him get a good breath of air (sometimes it takes as long as thirty seconds, and you will need to put your other hand under his tummy to support him), let him go under the water again, then bring him up again. Gradually let him come up more and more times as the lessons proceed. But be sure he has had a good breath between the submersions. You know yourself how uncomfortable and sometimes frightening it is to run out of air under the water.

Notice in this picture how the water is starting to swirl around toward the back of the pupil. It will then swish toward him and push him forward. This is an excellent way to teach him balance.

When he has progressed to the point where he can come up three or four times (with your help, of course), begin walking backward a little faster. The speed will cause the water to swirl around behind him and help push him along. Here is an excellent way to teach him balance. If you have ever shot a bow and arrow, you know how much farther and straighter the arrow goes without wobbling the farther back you pull the bow. Somehow this same principle helps a bicycle to balance and steadies your tiny student.

When he is able to swim in this manner for about fifteen feet, begin to combine his swimming *to* you with his swimming to the step, going away from you. Hold him around the waist and pull him at your side to a place where you can give him a push to the step.

Now he is really beginning to swim!

As the lessons progress, try letting him stay under longer before bringing him up. A few children can stay under for as long as a minute, but most can't hold their breath that long. You must watch for the signs of his wanting to come up. Some children will move their heads from side to side as though they are shaking them "no." Some infants will blow out all their air; still others start moving their arms and legs faster.

As the child becomes used to having you pull up on his chin, you will notice that he will anticipate your action by trying to put his head up by himself so that you will not have to put as much pressure on his chin.

And as he anticipates your pulling his chin, put as little pressure on his chin as possible.

You will also notice now that it won't take as long for him to get his breath of air. In anticipation of his coming out of the water, he will instinctively ready himself to breathe out and grab a bite of air. Don't try to teach him this breath control. You'll only be wasting your time, because he will control his own breathing when he is physically and mentally ready to do so.

This series of pictures shows how to bring a baby up from under the water to get air. Notice that the eleven-month-old grabs and holds my hand for security, but the "older" two-year-old does not.

When the child begins to learn to recover, he will first bring his head up with just his eyes above the water. Soon he'll be able to bring his nose out, then come up all the way. When he needs it, of course, you will assist him. His knowing you are right there to help will encourage him to try.

As time goes on, just a tap on the chin will cause him to raise his head to get a breath of air. Begin to let him stay under the water as long as possible—being careful to watch for signs of his running out of breath. But at this point you should wait until he *needs* to come up to get a breath, which will give him the incentive to *want to come up on his own.*

Don't be surprised at how long some children can hold air. By this time you should be able to tell just about how long your tiny charge is capable of staying under the water without discomfort.

When the child can recover by himself, begin gradually to get out of the water and stay out of the water during his lessons. In this way you can avoid his becoming psychologically attached to you.

However, don't suddenly stay out of the water one day when he no longer needs you. I begin by first sitting on the step at the end of the lesson while he plays, then on the side of the pool. Little by little, I stay out of the water more during the lesson. Then one day I busy myself with something beside the pool when his lesson should begin and say, "I'll be busy here for a minute, but you can go on in if you want to. I'll be right here." He'll go in the water without giving it a thought.

Now you've got yourself a swimmer!

FACING: This series of pictures shows how an infant comes from under the water to the surface to get air. Notice how she uses her hands to pull through the water and help bring her head up.

PART THREE

Side Lights

8

Floating

What good is it to learn to float? Well, for one thing, any skill a person (young or old) can learn in the water, the better swimmer he will be. Moreover, as a child gets older and swims longer distances, he will have the ability to float on his back to rest if he becomes tired. Such a respite can give the recuperation needed to resume a long swim to the safety of the shore.

Anyway, it's fun!

FACE-DOWN FLOATING

You won't need to teach a child to float on his face. At a certain point he will float naturally by himself. One day when he is swimming to you or to the steps, he won't move his arms or legs. He'll just float face down. This time comes when he is completely secure in the water and has complete confidence in you. (Remember when he automatically kicked his feet when you submerged him?)

Note to Parents: Although your baby will have confidence in *you from the beginning*, he won't reach this state of floating until he feels secure in the water.

When he does this, the first reaction is: "What's the matter? Has he forgotten how to swim?" No, he hasn't forgotten how to swim—he has taught himself to float! Don't discourage his floating, because this is a step forward for him. Encourage him with: "That's wonderful, Billy. You can float now." Children love the feeling of being suspended in the water without moving.

When he has discovered this enjoyable skill, he may want to do nothing else for a couple of lessons. Go ahead and let him, because he'll get used to it and come back to swimming later.

BACK FLOATING

When I first started teaching infants to swim, I could see no need to teach them to float on their backs and therefore didn't.

Then when Mary Frances Crosby wasn't yet two years old and had accomplished all the other skills required to pass the Beginner's Test of the American National Red Cross, I decided to try to teach her to float on her back. It was quite easy, because Mary Frances possessed exceptional co-ordination and balance. She went on, as I have said, to become the youngest swimmer in the history of the Red Cross to pass the Beginner's Test.

I was then inspired to try teaching other very young children to float on their backs, with interesting results. First I found that it was rather easy and then I discovered it helped them to learn to recover.

The important thing in this type of floating is to have the head back in a position so that the chest is up—followed by the hips and then the feet.

Be sure to stand behind the infant in a way that your body shades his face from the sun.

Since this is an awkward position for the child to assume, I knew that a game must be made of it. The game I call "I can see you upside down" is very effective.

I usually start teaching back floating when the child knows me reasonably well and before he has taught himself to float on his face, regardless of his age.

Some time during the lesson—it doesn't matter when—start teaching back floating by putting one hand behind the child's head just above the back of the neck and the other hand under the lower part of his back just above the waist. At the same time, stand behind and smile, saying: "I can see you upside down." He will hang onto your arms. At first this action is momentary. He will try to raise himself up. So don't force him to be on his back. As time goes on, he will become used to the position.

This is the first step in teaching the infant to float on his back. Support him under the shoulders in a way to shade his face. Here David raises a foot to balance himself because he still feels awkward in this position.

This is the proper position in which to hold the child's head while teaching the back float. My fingers are holding her chin up, my thumbs are supporting her head, and I am standing behind her so that the shadow of my body shades her face.

When he doesn't mind too much being on his back, he won't need the support beneath him, at least for a moment. Then you can use your free hand to touch his chin, nose, and eyes, and say, "I can see your chin upside down; I can see your nose upside down; I can see your eyes upside down." This game soon distracts him so that he isn't conscious of being on his back. As time goes on, use less lift in your support of him.

When he will float in this position for about ten seconds, momentarily release your support from under his head. Little by little, the time of the release increases, and he soon is floating on his own.

Up to this time you have been putting him in the position to float

As the infant develops confidence in floating on his back, only slight support under his head will need to be applied. By this time he will be used to facing the sun.

on his back. The next step is to show him how to push off from the side of the pool so that he can float by himself. The secret here is to teach him to push from the side *very gently,* so that he will not splash water in his face or sink under the water as he releases himself from the edge of the pool.

The child will have a tendency to try to push off and immediately put his face in the water in trying to float on his back. To avoid this habit, or to correct it, be sure that his head is back in position before he pushes from the side.

At the same time, encourage him to become accustomed to being on his back. Make a game of sitting on the top step of the shallow end of the pool and kicking the feet. Then gradually get him to lie farther back until he will be on his back, kicking. I usually play the "Animal" game as he kicks.

You will notice that when he has developed this new skill, his other skills will be improved also.

9

Jumping and Diving

It takes very little time for an infant to learn to jump and dive into the water—not more than two lessons to jump, and perhaps three or four to dive.

It is especially easy if the child has seen other children jumping and diving into the water. One day when I was teaching our eight-year-old neighbor, Terry, to dive, I took our little Patty along to watch. She was then just eighteen months old and had never been submerged in the water.

She sat interestedly watching on the other side of the deep end of the pool. She watched Terry put his hands over his head, put his head down and one foot up and slip into the water. After he had dived a couple of times, she went to the edge of the pool and imitated Terry perfectly, slithering into the water as though she had been diving a long time. I dived in after her to meet her at the bottom, and as I was going down, I wondered what her reaction would be. When she saw me coming, she smiled and stretched her hands out to me. When we surfaced I could see she was a little startled by the experience but thought it was great fun.

Here is the proper way to jump into the water while holding a small child. Notice that I am holding his head securely against mine, and that my legs are slightly separated so that we will not descend into the water too rapidly.

Holding the child's hand the first few times he jumps into the water will give him the confidence he needs to jump in unassisted.

That is how easy it is for little ones to learn to dive. One of the things that make learning to dive so easy is lack of fear. As a child gets older, the element of fear enters, and he is more reluctant to try.

One word of caution: Don't let small boys jump or dive into the water when they are nude. Although they are not likely to injure themselves, it could be painful.

I have found that it is better to teach children first to jump and then to dive into the water. Don't try to teach them both at the same time.

And remember: *Diving is for deep water only.*

JUMPING

Stand the child on the edge of the shallow end of the pool while you stand in the water in front of him. Hold him around the rib cage (he will automatically put his hands on your arms) and say: "One, two, three, four; Billy jumps in the pool," and gently pull him into the water without putting him under. (Not that he would be frightened, but he should have just one new experience at a time.) After he jumps in like this a couple of times, then let him submerge all the way.

The next step is to let go of him momentarily when he is under the water; then bring him up, as you did when you were first submerging him at the beginning. Now hold him by the hands to pull him into the water, instead of by the rib cage. Soon he should be ready to jump in the water alone. Then you can recover him (under the chin) when he is submerged. Shortly after, he'll automatically come up on his own.

The first few times he goes into the deep water, I hold him in my arms and jump in with him. One word of caution here: Hold him in your arms; he will put his arms around you; then *secure his head against yours as you go into the water.* It will prevent the water from knocking your heads together when you enter it. I don't need to tell you that such a collision can be painful.

Later, when the infant is used to going down deep in the water, he will be ready to try going down by himself. He, of course, won't go down as deep as you did, because he doesn't have enough weight. For this reason, some children like to have you hold them while they jump even after they are capable of jumping alone.

Use the following sequence. (You will have to be the judge of how many repeats to use for each stage, but generally speaking two or three jumps in each step will be enough.)

1. Hold his hand as you jump in the water with him.

2. Then hold his hand but let go of it when you are on the way down through the water.

3. Next, sit on the side, taking his hand to guide him into the water. When he is under, slip into the water and recover him. Don't jump or dive in. It roughens the water too much.

4. Now he is ready for you to wait for him in the pool, treading water in front of him and going under as he jumps to bring him back up. *Caution: Don't try to catch him when he jumps*. If this is necessary, he isn't ready for the deep water yet. And don't be too close—he might jump on you. You'll be surprised how far out some of these little kids can jump—especially the enthusiastic ones.

Little by little, he will be able to surface alone.

As soon as he is able to recover by himself in swimming, he will surface and swim on his own without you in the water.

DIVING

The simplest way to teach an infant to dive is to show him, getting him to imitate you. Here is the advantage of his watching other children. If he is used to seeing other children dive, he will want to dive too. If he hasn't had the opportunity to see other children, you'll have to demonstrate. To show him, put your hands on your head, bend over at the waist as far as you can, and fall in the water. Notice that this is *not* the way you teach an older child to dive.

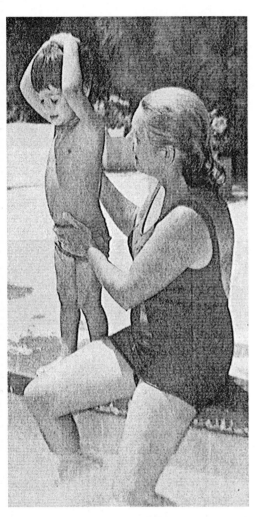

Here two-year-old David is assisted into the water several times before he tries to dive by himself. This is just a fall-in dive, and is not the Red Cross method of teaching diving.

Here eleven-month-old David is coaxed to "dive" into the water. This type of diving is for babies who can't yet walk.

The reason for putting your hands on your head is that a baby's arms are so short that they barely reach beyond his head, and since you want him to imitate you, you must demonstrate only what he is capable of imitating.

If the child is approaching three years, you can also show him how to raise one foot behind him as he dives. You can accomplish this by raising it up over his head as he falls bent over and hands over head.

When he has submerged and begins to lose momentum, he will instinctively start moving his arms and kicking his feet to come back to the surface.

For this age group you should not try to use the Red Cross method of teaching diving. That method is wonderful, and I, as a qualified Red Cross instructor, use it myself—but only for older children. You must keep all your teaching of little ones in the stage of their imitating you—and as simple as possible.

10

Water Safe—What Next?

As I said earlier, a child is completely water safe—meaning that he can propel himself about in the water without needing someone to be in the water with him—when he can accomplish all the skills required to pass the American National Red Cross Beginner's Test. And as a review I will repeat them here. He can:

> Swim at least fifteen feet;
> Recover (come up to get a breath of air);
> Float on his back at least ten seconds;
> Jump into deep water;
> Dive into deep water.

In some instances—in a lake or ocean—he won't have learned to jump and dive, but there he won't need to.

There are various degrees of safety, however. In my opinion, a child is reasonably safe the minute he is capable of paddling several feet in the water so that he could protect himself if he fell or was pushed into the water.

Age has much to do with a child's ability to save himself in the water. I don't claim that a baby of four, six, or even eight months could save himself. He might be able to propel himself to the edge of the pool, but I doubt that he would have the ability to pull himself out of the water. But a year-old child could! So why take the trouble to start teaching an eight-month-old baby to swim? Because by the time a child reaches the age of walking, he is in danger around water, and it will take several months of water experience to reach the point where he can be completely safe.

By "completely safe," I do *not* mean that he could or should be left alone near water for even a minute. Just as *any person, young or old, should never swim alone.* Although you will not have to be in the water with him, someone should always be in the area, and watching.

It is best to explain this to a child's parents when he has reached this point of water safety. Many parents don't realize the potential dangers of swimming alone and would not hesitate to let the small child swim by himself.

You should also explain to the parent that two small children shouldn't swim alone together either. A responsible older child or adult should be in the pool area with the infant at all times. My rule of thumb for the protection of very small children is that the "responsible older child" must be at least twelve years old and have a Junior Life Saving Certificate.

When the infant is water safe and can flit about on his own like a little tadpole, what comes next? Nothing! I have found that it is best to let the child have nothing but fun with his newly accomplished skills for a long time. The natural reaction is to start a child on the formal strokes, such as the crawl or backstroke. But a little child is not interested in learning any more than he knows now; he just wants to enjoy the water. And why not? He will continue developing co-ordination and balance by using just the little dog-paddle stroke he now knows until he is old enough for organized instruction.

If children are pushed too hard, they only develop a strong hatred

After the lesson comes the milk break. Here is ten-month-old David, who cannot yet feed himself but can swim well enough to save himself if he happened
to fall into the water.

for the water. A little boy I had in one of my classes at Black-Foxe Military School experienced this very thing. He had taken lessons since he was two years old, and at six he was an excellent and beautiful swimmer, but he hated the water. Every class swimming day he came up with a different excuse for why he couldn't go in the water. Finally I got a little exasperated with him, and said, "Kevin, I can't excuse you from swimming unless you bring me a note from your mother!"

The next day he gave me a piece of paper which, in first-grade printing, said: "From mother—No Swim." When I read that note, I could have cried. Here was a boy who, instead of loving the water as all boys should, had a deep underlying hatred of it.

After discussing the incident, the athletic director, his parents, and I decided to let Kevin exchange another activity for swimming. When I left the school five years later this young boy still didn't swim, because somehow he'd had enough swimming to last him a lifetime.

So explain to the parents that their infant will have a better chance of making the Olympic team if he isn't pushed. Most parents want to do what's best for their child.

What happens at the end of the summer season? If the child can continue swimming during the winter months, as we do here in Southern California, that's wonderful. However, in many parts of the country there are no indoor pools available. Will the child have forgotten by next summer? What can be done to help him during the long winter months until he can be in the water again?

Some schools substitute another athletic program for swimming in the wintertime. If this is the case, part of the program can be a game or games of pretending they're swimming while lying or running around the floor. Children love to pretend. If you have a mirror in the gym, all the better. Pretending to swim does two things. First, it provides an opportunity to continue developing the co-ordination it takes to swim. Second, it keeps the mental picture of swimming in the child's mind, helping him anticipate with joy the coming summer, when he can go back into the water.

If the school doesn't have a winter schedule, encourage the parents to work in the above manner with their child.

A parent can also be encouraged to let the child play in the bathtub, getting his face and head under the water. If the tub is filled about three quarters full, there is enough water in it for the child to have lots of fun. Poker chips can be used here also.

But please warn the parent not to leave a very young child alone in the bathtub even if he is as water safe as he can get for his age. He could slip and fall or have a dozen other accidents.

The following summer, if you haven't seen the child all through the winter months, and even if his parents have worked with him, be sure to take a few lessons to get reacquainted with him. Remember, he will have grown a lot and he will have had many new experiences in the interim. So take it easy at first and let it all come back to him gradually.

11

Safety First, Last, and Always

From the first minute of the first lesson, stress safety first, last, and always. *Children should not be allowed to develop habits that are safe for them now but would be unsafe at a later date.* For instance, a small child should not be taught or allowed to dive into the shallow water, because this experience establishes a habit he must not practice when he is older and bigger. Always remember that he is forming swimming habits (good or bad) that he will use the rest of his life.

I know of a seventeen-year-old champion swimmer who dived through an inner tube and struck the inside edge in a way that broke his neck. Yet I see children doing this very thing (and sometimes being encouraged to do so by well-meaning adults) every day without realizing the real danger involved.

In connection with safety rules, another thing that should not be allowed is horseplay. Although this problem at times isn't a big one, it should not be allowed to get started. Sometimes little sister is allowed to push bigger brother (who can swim) into the water. Since children in the age group we are dealing with have no judgment at all, they could very easily push a nonswimmer into the pool.

Over the years there has been no lack of spectacular examples of the dangers of horseplay. Another champion I knew, with a couple of other boys, was trying to see how close he could come to a drain outlet in a huge city-owned pool that was being drained without being sucked into it. Here is Russian roulette under water! And in this strong young man's case, his misfortune was complete. The rapid current wedged his body into the drain entrance, and the others were unable to free him before his breath was exhausted.

Children should be taught from the beginning that they will *never* become such good swimmers that it is impossible to drown. Nobody can.

In teaching little ones, you might want to substitute something for the poker chips. The substitution in itself is all right, but don't use small coins, pennies, nickels, dimes, or quarters. As you know, infants put everything and anything into their mouths, and these small coins are very easily swallowed. For the same reason, don't use marbles. In addition, marbles will rapidly roll to the deepest part of the pool. (However, it is fun for older boys and girls to see if they can catch them before they stop rolling.)

As silly as it may sound, small children should not be allowed to touch each other while they are in the water. It is a simple procedure for two or three small ones to drown each other. They get so used to hanging onto the teacher that they naturally grab anyone else around unless you teach them not to. An exception to this rule is in organized play such as "Ring around the rosies." And, of course, in that event, the teacher is present.

One day, at a San Fernando Valley Swimming School pool, the instructor turned his back for a moment while a couple of two-year-olds were together in the water. In front of the concentrated gaze of a half-dozen mothers—not one of whom could understand what was happening—the two clinched like prize fighters and began to strangle. I jumped in the pool after them and had them out of the water before their instructor turned around.

He said: "I've told those kids not to do that!"

But the time element is too brief for hindsight to help. Don't ever turn your back on your tiny charges. Mistakes in this area are irreversible.

On the subject of diving, in my opinion small children should not be allowed to dive from great heights. Even a ten-foot board is too high. Since infants have no control over their bodies in the air, they could land flat on the water, which is the least of the mishaps possible. The impact upon hitting the surface of the water fast is so great that they might twist a neck, pull a muscle in one of their arms, or, even worse, sprain their backs.

I admit that accidents such as these in diving are rare, but they are possible, and I don't allow my small charges to take chances.

It's very spectacular to see an eighteen-month-old baby diving from a ten-foot board, I know. But we aren't teaching these little ones to swim for sensationalism; we're teaching them for safety's sake. And happiness.

If a child has a mishap around the pool area (providing it isn't a serious accident), take him into the water and play for a few minutes so he won't remember the experience in connection with swimming. One day while Harry Crosby was waiting for Mary Frances to finish her lesson, he fell over a small table that was beside a lawn chair. The fall knocked the wind out of him, and he fainted. When he regained consciousness, I could see that he was not otherwise physically injured, and I coaxed him into the water. In just a few minutes the color came back into his face and he had a short but a fun lesson, and the unfortunate incident was never thought of again. It's the old story of getting back on the horse after a fall.

A child who cannot yet swim but has *no fear of the water* is in a very dangerous position. To those of you who teach in private homes: Remember that it is your responsibility to see that the pool area is left locked and otherwise safe when the lesson is over and you leave the pool. Make that your unvarying responsibility, even if the parent says, "Don't bother to lock it; we're going in after a while."

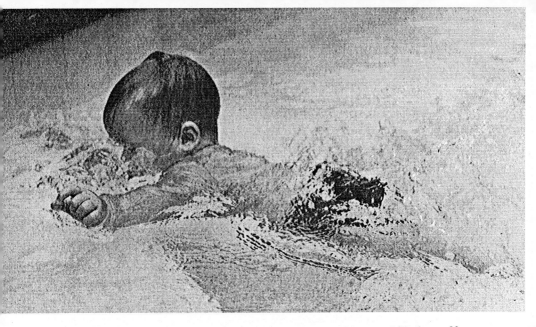

This series of pictures shows how an infant can be taught to paddle himself to the steps and safety even though he is not able to "recover." He should also be taught to paddle to all the other edges of the pool where it is possible for him to fall in.

And to you parents who are teaching your own baby in your own pool: *Always lock the gate, even if you plan to use the pool within a few minutes.* Many things can change that plan without advance notice. Most of the tragic accidents have occurred in otherwise normal circumstances with the fatal flaw of a few minutes (sometimes only a matter of seconds) of inattention. Callers ring the doorbell as if by fate, or the phone rings at just the wrong distracting moment. One mother who met misfortune said she had just smelled her food burning on the stove and run to cope with it.

Don't always blame the pool. In the same manner, the family bathtub claims many hundreds more victims every year.

Always keep in mind that a gate can be unlocked but a child cannot be "undrowned." How many parents wish they could!

FACING: These pictures show how an infant can pull himself to safety even though he cannot yet come up to get a breath of air.

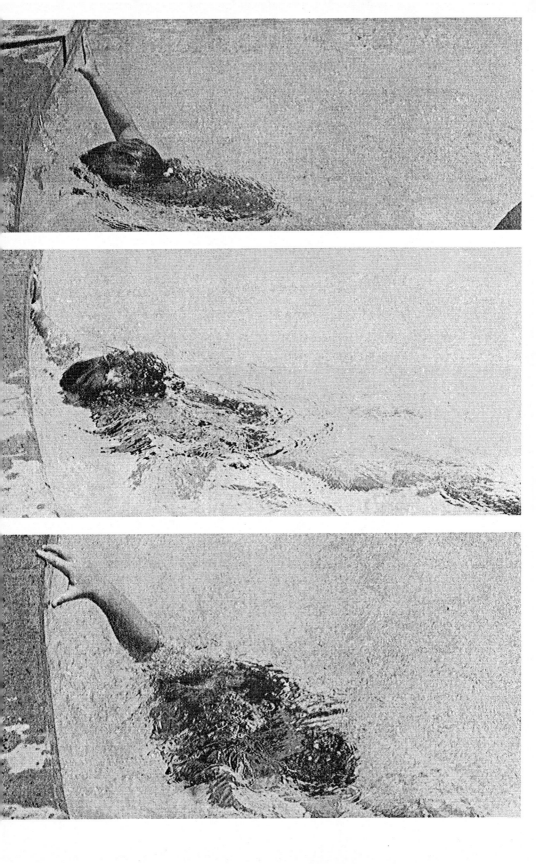

12

Games

A major aid in teaching an infant to swim—and one you can be resourceful in making into a most helpful tool for your kit—is games. Since a child in this youngest age group cannot take direct instruction, games do the teaching for you. And they make it fun for him. For that reason, be sure to enter into activities with the child. For instance, when you play the "Ring around the rosies" game, always go under water with the child.

Although I will discuss games all children like to play, the games individual children like most are the ones that affect them personally. When I started to teach John Wayne's son Ethan to swim, he had just returned from Lima, Peru, where he had been visiting his maternal grandmother. I floated a toy airplane out into the water, and Ethan swam out to it, pretending that he was on it going back to Lima to visit his grandmother.

In this way, you can use any happy occasion that a child has experienced to make up a game that suits him personally.

One thing that is of great assistance is to keep an open mind and listen. No matter how much you know about swimming, you can always learn more—and often from someone who knows nothing or very little about swimming. A parent taught me a game, "Bubbles," that he played with his little son, Matthew. If you put your hand flat on top of the water and very rapidly push it down into the water next to the child, little air bubbles will form, and these bubbles tickle. Now that is something only a man would think of.

I usually play "Bubbles" to help a child get acquainted with the water. The pleasant feeling of being tickled on legs and body makes a happy association with the water.

"Peek-a-boo" is a game many infants already know and is a good one to help establish a rapport with him. Put your face in the water and come up saying "peek-a-boo." He will often imitate you immediately.

All children love balloons. To give the balloons a little weight so they can be better controlled, I fill the deflated balloon with water, then blow it up to the desired size. Beach balls are a little too heavy and awkward for infants to try to handle.

Older boys and girls like to use the balloons to play water volleyball; as a matter of fact, so do some adults. This makes a good family game.

To help make the lessons fun and make the whole surrounding area one that seems pleasant to the child, I use parts of the pool itself to play games. When you take him on the little adventures around the pool, stop at all the interesting places, such as the underwater lights. Children enjoy going down into the water to feel the lights. First take them down (after counting one, two, three, four); later, when they are more experienced, they may want to go down without your holding them. On the sides, under the water, many pools have relief figures of fish, which children also like to explore. Figures on the bottom of the pool encourage children to go down, too. These are just a few examples; there are dozens of things in pools that children love to see.

And, if I may repeat myself, this is a wonderful way to help the child become acquainted with the area in which he swims. It is particularly important if he is learning in his own pool, where he has more chance to fall in the water when no one is around.

Pushing your hands rapidly through the water makes bubbles, which tickle and are fun.

Given the opportunity, most children will make up their own games.

When the child has advanced to the stage where he can flutter kick, as a diversion and to keep the lessons interesting, I play with him the "Animal" game, which was described on page 53. This game will also keep your own thighs, hips, and tummy under control.

Children love to slide. On the first trips down the sliding board it is best to hold the child's hand for security. If he isn't able to recover yet, I then slip into the pool to get him. Don't jump in, because it will make too big a splash and he could get a mouthful of water when you pull him to the surface.

The life-saving ring with a rope can be used. When the child has progressed to the stage at which he can swim on his own for about ten seconds and has good balance (it isn't necessary for him to be able to

Playing in a ring buoy is helpful *and* fun.

recover), I let him hold onto the rings as I walk along the edge of the pool and pull him through the water with the rope. *Be sure to watch him in case he lets go or tips over.*

"Submarine" is a game children like to play. Let the child hang onto your shoulders as you swim breast stroke. Say "submarine," and then go under, come up; then repeat. When he gets the idea of the game, let him guide it himself by saying "submarine" when he wants to go under.

Although not a game in itself, children like to see what I call the "magic ball." If you push a rubber beach ball down into the water as far as you can and then release it quickly, it will "jump" up out of the water. I have found this a wonderful distraction for children who are a little shy about the water at first. It helps them realize that the water is fun and fascinating.

Children get a big kick out of seeing a real dog swim and *love to imitate it.* There was great excitement the day Bing Crosby brought one of his hunting dogs, a beautiful Labrador retriever, over to the pool. He threw a stick out into the pool for the dog to retrieve, and ever after, the children imitated the dog's response.

Ethan Wayne had a little dog that followed him wherever he went, and the day his older sister, Aissa, put the dog in the water, he jumped up and down and squealed with delight when he saw his favorite puppy swimming. And then he always wanted the dog to swim with him. (This is against the health laws for public pools and for some beaches, so it can be practiced only in the privacy of home pools.)

I was amused by an incident that happened to a friend who is one of our country's greatest swim coaches and who has trained many national and Olympic champions.

A Beverly Hills dowager approached him with her miniature poodle, Isabel, and asked him if he would teach her dog to swim. She was afraid her pet would fall into their family pool and drown. He did a double take as he looked from her worried face to the beady-eyed manicured bundle in her arms.

After taking a deep breath, he said: "Sure, for forty bucks a lesson!"

He thought that price was so high she would refuse. But nothing was too good for her little Isabel. That may be one of the highest prices anyone has paid for swimming lessons—especially for a pupil who didn't need them in the first place.

I have told you about just a few of the games I use. The possibilities are endless, and the more personal and original you are, the more fun the child will have.

However, don't try to use too many different kinds of games at one time. Pick a few favorite ones to use. Then every once in a while try a new game. Too many different kinds of activities in one lesson will confuse the infant. Keep the lessons and games simple.

13

Fear

Although most children you will teach in this age group will have no fear, you have to face the fact that you'll run across a child every once in a while who is afraid. The question for you is: Where did his fear come from—a bad experience or bad conditioning—and what can you do about it?

If at all possible, try to find out what has made the child fearful. About ninety-nine per cent of the time it won't be the water itself.

A couple of examples come to my mind. One is of a little two-year-old girl who had been taught by someone who forced her to swim, and every time she cried the teacher ducked her under the water. Her mother said that Mary Ann started to cry when they got in the car to go to the swim school, and later got to the point where she vomited every time she got in the car whether or not they were going swimming. (She was still vomiting whenever she got in the car six months later, even though meanwhile I had taught her successfully to swim.) What the mother had thought was going to be a delightful experience had turned out to be a nightmare. So I decided on an alternate approach.

The family didn't have a pool themselves, and since I didn't want Mary Ann to associate the car with swimming any more, I asked the mother to borrow the use of a pool within walking distance of their home. One of their neighbors was nice enough to oblige.

We started from the beginning. I asked the mother to come in the water with us, and I was very careful not to do anything that would give Mary Ann a chance to repeat a traumatic experience.

It took a little longer to teach Mary Ann, but it paid off, because today—nearly three years later—swimming is Mary Ann's favorite pastime.

The other experience I remember is a personal one and shows that even when you use every precaution, a child can have a bad experience. One day in the pool, after I had been teaching seventeen-month-old Craig to swim for about three months, a sudden earth-shattering noise came from next door. Someone was cutting down a tree with a power saw. Craig started screaming hysterically, and, of course, I removed him from the water immediately. Don't forget that fear of loud noises is one of the things babies are born with.

At the next lesson he refused to go into the water with me alone. I asked his mother to come in the pool with us, and from then on she or his older brother swam with us. The presence of his mother or brother helped him get over the hump without this unfortunate incident becoming the source of a trauma.

If an unfortunate incident occurs while you are teaching, be sure to make every effort possible to disassociate it from swimming. I have found that the presence of the mother or another member of the family in the water with you will usually do the trick.

Even when teaching older children, I have always made it a point to keep the child from experiencing anything unpleasant connected with swimming.

George was about three and a half when I started giving him swimming lessons. He had been cautioned many times to stay out of and away from the deep end of the pool. So when he could swim across the shallow end of the pool and it was time for us to try the deep water, George was afraid. I could see by the look on his face that it was real fear (some of these little characters are fakers, you know), so I said, "It's okay, George; you don't have to swim in the deep today. Maybe you'll feel like it tomorrow." The next day George came wearing a dollar-sized St. Christopher's medal around his neck, and when I asked him if he wanted to try the deep water, he went to the edge of the deep end, stopped, looked down at his medal for a moment, jumped in the water, and swam all the way across the pool.

When your small pupil is able to come up to get a breath of air by himself and you no longer need to be in the water with him, if he should happen to get into a little trouble, don't go in the water after him unless it is absolutely necessary. Instead, coax him to the edge of the pool by talking to him: "Kick and pull, Johnny; you can make it," and hold out your hand to assist him psychologically. Then praise him: "That was great! I knew you could do it!" He will be very proud.

If you go in the water after him, it will frighten him, because he will think he couldn't make it. These little ones are a lot smarter than you think they are.

From my own personal experience, I am convinced that many of the fears children have of the water are a result of well-meaning people who rescued them from "drowning" when there was no need to.

A classic example of this occurred one day at our church camp, Cedar Lake. A number of teen-agers were scuffling in the water over a greased watermelon—you know the game—when one of the girls ran out of air under water and when she came up she got a mouthful of water, which is rather frightening, and she started to struggle a little. One of the counselors who was observing on the sideline dived in after her even though it wasn't necessary. She was fine for about five minutes and then she started thinking about the incident and became hysterical, because she thought she had almost drowned, and she was too afraid to go back in the water all summer. She will probably always be afraid of the water, for no good reason.

The same is true of small children. Even though they forget the incident itself, there is always that underlying and unexplainable fear.

Don't let them drown, but think twice before you rush to give them unnecessary aid.

14

Hard-to-Control Children

As in any other age group of children, you will, from time to time, come across a child who is very difficult to control.

These children usually have parents who have been either over-indulgent or overly strict.

A two-year-old boy comes to my mind who was the son of a man said to be powerful in the underworld. When I went to their beautiful mansion in Los Angeles the first time, I took a little water toy with me to help smooth the way in getting acquainted. Although the father was friendly to me, he said, "Please don't bring him toys." Then he added, "We don't intend to pay him for learning to swim; it's costing a helluva lot of dough for these lessons, and, by God, he'd better appreciate it without being paid!"

The father sat beside the pool during every lesson and watched. Sure enough, little Cliff tried very hard to do everything I asked him to. At the end of each lesson he would say, "Did I obey you? Did I obey you?" And, of course, I assured him that he had.

Then one day his father was not at the lesson because he had gone out of town on business. To my amazement, Cliff was a changed child. He would do nothing I asked him to.

I didn't want to use his father as a threat—I could see that he was already afraid enough of him—and his father refused to let me reward him, so I teased and coaxed him into having somewhat of a lesson. When the father returned, the lessons resumed as usual. We continued in this manner until Cliff became a safe swimmer.

I could have used force and overpowered him. But I have found that it is best to keep the child on your side. If he likes you, he will like swimming, and it will be easier for you in the long run.

Another type of child is the overindulged one. As with older children like this, you must be *friendly* but *firm*.

It is better to say, "It is time to . . ." and never "Do you want to . . . ." Children in this "terrible two's" age group will automatically say "no" even if they mean yes.

Then sometimes you get into the problem of "No, I don't want to kick on the steps! I want to play 'Ring around the rosies.'" *Don't give in.* Say, "Fine, we'll play 'Ring around the rosies' *after* we kick on the steps." And stick to it. If you give in once, you start a battle of wits. As I have said before, two-year-olds are very shrewd, and it doesn't take them long to figure you out and know exactly where they stand.

I'm talking here about the hard-to-control child, not the timid little girl who says, "May we play 'Ring around the rosies' first?" In that case, I always comply with her wishes.

Never threaten a hard-to-control child with "I'm going to tell your mother." In the first place, he already has control of his mother, and in the second place, you weaken your own position by suggesting that you have lost control of him. And don't think they don't love this.

I also use incentive for these children by giving a material reward. There is on the market striped gum that comes in different colors in each package. After a lesson in which the child has co-operated, I let him have a choice of which stick of gum he wants.

You can also use the little bubble-gum machines and give them a penny to get the gum ball.

Some parents don't like their children to have gum, and some in this

We hope there's one more left! Reward is a powerful weapon.

age group have never tasted it. In that case I use other things; for example, I let them dry on my "magic" blue towel or take a ride in my "magic" red car.

One thing that is very important is not to give a reward unless the child has really earned it. If you do, you again easily risk losing control.

The use of these tactics may seem as though you are rewarding the difficult child, but not the co-operative one. Well-disciplined and well-behaved children in this age group don't need rewards other than praise. Praise is enough for them. Though from time to time, I take them a little water toy, "just because I like you."

15

Lakes, Oceans, and Beaches

Up to now I have talked mostly about pool swimming. Unfortunately, we don't all have modern heated swimming pools to teach our babies to swim in. However, there are other bodies of water in which an infant can and does play and therefore could learn to swim.

For instance, not long ago a man asked me if a little child could learn to swim in Long Island Sound. And I said that he could.

I've never seen Long Island Sound, but I know that a child could learn to swim in this dog-paddle way in *any* body of water that he would ordinarily play in, if it's deep enough. You couldn't, for example, teach him to swim in one of those little plastic pools that are only a couple of inches deep. Larger ones, however, are suitable.

The most important thing to teach an infant—coming up to get a breath of air—can just as easily be taught in lakes or other still water as in a pool. All other phases of teaching can be improvised to suit the situation.

In my opinion, an infant is far better off if he is taught to swim in the same body of water that he is going to swim in for pleasure. So if you are at the beach, the preference would be to teach him or have him taught at the place where he swims instead of taking him elsewhere to a pool to learn.

There are some things you probably won't be able to teach an infant in a lake or at the sea—for instance, diving or jumping into water over his head—but then there is no immediate need to.

On the other hand, there are some advantages to teaching at these places.

One advantage of natural bodies is that the temperature of the water remains more nearly constant. Even though ocean or lake water is colder than water in a pool, the child can accustom himself to it, and there won't be sudden changes, as there are in pools when the heater goes off or after a very cold night. Another advantage is that the infant has a wonderful opportunity to sit at the edge of the water where it is only an inch deep and gradually go into the deeper water. (Pools are not constructed like this, my husband tells me, because it would take up too much room and would be too expensive; we have to use steps instead.)

Overcoming the awkward feeling of floating is much easier on a beach than it is in a pool, because the child won't mind so much lying on his back in the very shallow water.

Also, the child can be taught to put his face in the water easily in very shallow water. As he sits and plays or runs, he will eventually fall over and get his face wet anyway. You, of course, laugh and pretend that it was a game he made up. I often use this method purposely when there are steps in a pool long enough and shallow enough. It works especially well with children who haven't quite made up their minds whether they like having water in their faces.

There are conditions, of course, that do exist in these areas that are not present in pools.

In the first place, since the water itself is usually considerably colder, the child must gradually build a resistance to it. But it is quite simple to take the child in for five minutes three, four, or five times a day to accomplish this.

112

There is, also, sometimes rough water. It is, as far as I know, impossible (no, difficult—few things are impossible) to teach anyone to swim in rough water. But I would imagine that a child wouldn't be tempted to go near rough water either, and he certainly wouldn't be playing in it.

If the water is usually calm and becomes rough or in any way unlike that in which he is used to swimming (full of seaweed, dirt, etc.), cancel the lesson just as you would in pools when the water suddenly becomes cold.

Some beaches are rocky and hurt children's feet when they can't wear beach walkers or go-aheads or whatever you call them. This happened to the Crosby children. Bing has a home down in a tiny village on the coast of Mexico, and although the water is very warm, the pebbles on the beach are so sharp that the children kept cutting their feet. I had a man who makes skin-diving equipment make them each a pair of rubber booties to wear to the water's edge. It seemed to work out pretty well. These booties should not be worn in the water, however.

In using the plastic types of pools, which bring water fun into our back yards, lessons can be improvised.

These pools vary in size; for successful teaching in this type of pool, the water should be at least two feet deep.

One definite advantage to teaching in a small pool like this is that the water can be kept very warm without having to use a heater.

Some of the very small pools are emptied every day or so and refilled. When refilling the pool, be sure to leave enough time for the sun to warm the water—usually a couple of hours—or fill it from the warm-water faucet if you don't have time to wait. Or drag out the whistling teakettle and add a bit of hot water (before you put the baby in).

There is no point in giving greater detail here. You the teacher know your own area of teaching far better than I do. The important thing is to follow the simple steps given in this book and improvise in your own knowledgeable way.

16

Review

In reviewing the preceding chapters I'll try to put the whole process of teaching an infant to swim in a "nutshell." First there are the Ten Commandments of teaching these little ones:

1. Don't underestimate the power of praise.
2. Give him your undivided attention.
3. Let him learn at his own pace.
4. Don't proceed when in doubt.
5. Remove him from the water if he cries.
6. Don't do anything to cause a traumatic experience.
7. Don't overexpose him to water.
8. Demonstrate only what he is capable of imitating.
9. Always be in control of him and of the situation.
10. Always keep a happy smile.

As you teach the infant to swim, always bear in mind that the main reason he is learning is for safety's sake—even though he is having fun in the process.

Be sure to establish a happy rapport with him. Take time to let him get acquainted with the surroundings and don't hesitate to invite the parents—especially the mother—to come into the water with you during the first "get-acquainted" lessons.

Be sure the infant is well acquainted with you and trusts you before you submerge him under the water. At first he is under the water only one half of a second; very gradually prolong the time he is under the water.

Take plenty of time in teaching him to come up to get a breath of air. Recovering is the most important single thing you will teach him, so be sure he has a good foundation of balance and co-ordination before you start this skill. Also be sure that he gets a good breath of air when you bring him up out of the water. When he is capable of coming up on his own, he will instinctively prepare himself so that he can stay up long enough to get air.

If possible, let him learn to jump and dive into the water by imitating someone near his own age.

Use the rope-and-towel harness only when the child is willing.

Keep the upper hand, especially with children who are hard to control.

Last, but far from least, always keep in mind the safety factor.

If you follow the suggestions I have put down here and use your own experiences and innovations, I know you will enjoy teaching these little children. They come to feel that you are their private possession, and as far as they are concerned, the lesson begins the minute they see you.

And always keep your aplomb—even as you learn to expect the unexpected.

A friend of mine who teaches in a swim school was a few minutes late one day for her first lesson with an eager two-year-old. When she started toward the dressing room little Melinda wanted to join her, so Caroline agreed to let her go along. Five minutes later when the two emerged from the bath house Melinda announced to the entire school: "Caroline wears purple pants!"

So have fun!

116

About the Author

Virginia Hunt Newman, known throughout the world as "the mother of infant swimming," was inducted in 1993 into the International Swimming Hall of Fame (ISHOF) and the National Swim School Association Hall of Fame. As chair of the World Aquatic Babies Congress, she travels to their conferences, which are conducted throughout the world.

Mrs. Newman lives in southern California and has two grown children and three grandchildren. In her spare time she volunteers at the Motion Picture and Television retirement home, is on the board of governors of ISHOF, and still teaches swimming to tiny pupils.

0-595-22324-9

Printed in the United States
35855LVS00006B/169-171